LIMITLESS MEMORY

Learn to use Advanced Strategies to Learn Faster and Remember More to be More Productive

L. C JINO

Copyright © 2019 by L.C Jino

All rights reserved.

No part of this book may be used or reproduced by any means, graphic, electronic, or mechanical, including photocopying, recording, taping, or by any information storage retrieval system, without the written permission of the publisher except in the case of brief quotations embodied in critical articles and reviews.

Table of Contents

INTRODUCTION 1

CHAPTER 1: CONCENTRATE 3

CHAPTER 2: EXCUSES 7

CHAPTER 3: DO NOT BELIEVE IN LIES 12

    A friendly advice 15

    How to Unlock your Inner Potential 15

CHAPTER 4: BE HERE AND NOW 18

    Five Rules 19

CHAPTER 5: CREATE AND CONNECT 22

CHAPTER 6: BRING INFORMATION TO LIFE 26

    The Process of Memory Encoding 28

    Transferring information from Short-Term Memory to Long-term Memory 30

CHAPTER 7: USE YOUR BODY TO REMEMBER 32

CHAPTER 8: PEGGING INFORMATION DOWN 35

    Process of Memory Consolidation 37

    Neurons and their Importance 37

Memory Retrieval 38

Chapter 9: Linking Thoughts 39

Direct Retrieval 39

Process of Memory Retrieval 40

Difference between Recognition and Recall 40

Process of Recall 42

Life Example 44

Secrets to Memorize Faster than Anyone 45

Chapter 10: Remembering Names 47

Effectively use of Left and Right Brain for Memorization 48

Ron White's Method 52

Harry Lorayne's Method 53

Chapter 11: Remember the Number 55

Memorizing the Pi 57

Method 1 – Grouping 57

Method 2 – Word & Sound Swap 58

Combination of Left & Right Brain for Better Memorization 59

Chapter 12: Art of Memory 61

Memory Palace Technique 61

Acronyms 64

The Method of Loci 65

    Other Useful Techniques 68

CHAPTER 13: THE METHODS I PERSONALLY USED & RECOMMEND 73

CHAPTER 14: SELF-DISCIPLINE 75

    Recommendation & Tips for Memorizing 76

CONCLUSION 78

INTRODUCTION

During the past years, I have told myself that I wanted to impart the special skill most people lack of which I am really proud of, I wished to be a part of their life transformation. This one skill that I have really mastered throughout the years of practicing which is having a fast & sharp memory.

Finally, it has come to this day that I am able to publish an eBook to share my unique skill which is not born with but through years and years of hard practicing to achieved my current state. Showing all the techniques which works for me and no doubt help each and everyone who read this eBook & keen to self-improve.

Spending several days and sleepless nights writing down all the knowledge that I have personally used which are effective and gain success from. "Limitless Memory: Learn to use Advanced Strategies to Learn Faster and Remember More to be More Productive" is an eBook for ones who wish to improve themselves, with a pure intention of helping people to enhance their memory.

Limitless Memory

I hope that you take the knowledge that I am imparting here in this eBook in good use for your future to learn easily and achieve a "limitless memory" which is the purpose of this eBook and my personal goal.

CHAPTER 1

Concentrate

Where you are. Be There!

As we all know it is very important to have a maximum concentration in everything that we do especially if it is crucial to our success and progress.

There are people who have unmatched skills when it comes to concentration maybe because it is their innate nature to have a deep focus in whatever they are doing thus resulting in a much better performance.

It is crucial in the sense that having good concentration skills improve not only our ability to think but also our personality as well. I have known a lot of people who have good concentration skills and most of them are really good at memorizing things. I was awed with their

Limitless Memory

abilities and I told myself back then that I should also have good concentration skills as them.

Thankfully, it was the trend of speedcubing back in the days (a sport in which you solve the Rubik's cube as fast as you can) and I became an avid fan of speed cubing and other types of puzzles.

This became the starting point of me building good concentration skills and eventually developed my memorization skills as well.

I was truly amazed that I have such ability that I haven't thought of before. When you are learning to solve the Rubik's cube you need to tremendously memorize all the algorithms (pattern) if you are really serious in progressing to a more professional way of solving.

So, I memorized all the algorithms and began to practice day and night. I am really eager and focus to reach my goals which is to become faster as well as to master all the algorithms.

This maybe the main reason why I became a hustler in concentration and eventually in memorizing things and speedcubing really helped me a lot.

Not all of us are interested in solving puzzles and I know that but this shall not be the reason why you shouldn't have a good concentration. As enhancing your concentration skills can be done in many ways.

Think of it as part of your inner self, as we all know driving requires all of concentration to avoid any road hazards or accidents to occur.

As you speed up, the deeper your concentration & awareness of your surrounding in order for you to react swiftly with great focus.

Having good concentration skills is a huge factor in how we can develop our memorization skills as well. I know you are aware of that! Let us take schooling as an example, remember when our teacher is telling us to study for an upcoming examination?

We tend to memorize a lot of terms and we can only successfully remember them if we put in extra focus & concentration. Sometimes we get distracted by something while studying and it frequently happens because our concentration is completely ruined which result in poor absorption of information. Have you ever noticed that? All of us came to a point in which we are easily distracted which compromises the task that we are doing.

Limitless Memory

Since I was a child, I am really enthusiastic about learning but I still tend to get distracted and lazy. Getting out of my comfort zone is hard but thanks to my mom as she was really patient towards me, in my discipline for my studies.

Don't be stress, even though you are not a fan of studies nor any strong fundamentals when you are a child, the memorizing techniques that you will learn in my eBook will still greatly help you in achieving a limitless memory.

CHAPTER 2

Excuses

You Cannot Continue to Fly with the Eagle If you Continue to Scratch with the Turkeys

Have you ever thought of the reason why you are having a hard time memorizing?

The main factor would be Excuses. It comes down to the question of how eager are you to improve yourself.

Simply because enhancing our memories requires discipline and hard work. There is no room for excuses if you really want to improve yourself. Bad habits such as laziness, lack of motivation, bad nutrition, and lifestyle have to be forcefully removed in order for you to succeed.

We can apply discipline in our everyday lives whenever we are doing something whether is our job or studying in school. Whenever we plan to do something, we always have this mindset of doing it later because we are used to be in the Comfort Zone, coming up with a lot of excuses which the primary reason is lack of self-discipline & laziness.

If you really want to improve…

First get out of your comfort zone and practice Self Discipline!

Limitless Memorization skills could only be achieved by proper Self-Discipline.

In order to help you get out of the comfort zone, here are some tips that greatly helped me in the past in becoming a fully self-disciplined individual.

It is proven to increase concentration which will help in you achieve a sharp memory.

> ➢ **Sleeping is essential**
>
>   What I personally do is I would lie down on my bed, clear my mind off any distractions that might distract my sleep. Those distraction consist of gadgets such as mobile phones, console games, tablets etc. We tend to look at them too frequently which results to sleepless nights and less than 7 hours of uninterrupted rest.

- ➢ **Reduce the usage of headphones**

    We all love music and we can't deny the fact that we listen to music very often using headphone. It is recommended to listen to music using a speaker but keep in mind that it is not advisable to listen to loud music as it could potentially damage your eardrums which is why you should keep the music at a tolerable volume.

- ➢ **Stop eating junk food, consume more healthy foods**

    Consuming lots of junk food such as snacks and sweetening drinks could decrease the level of concentration and focus. Glucose is like an ecstasy to the brain which cause it to get hyperactive in a short time, leaving the rest of your time restless & tired. But that doesn't mean that you do not consume any sweetening food. Your brain feed on glucose as nutrients. Junk food are harmful to our body, as it stresses out your kidneys and inflame your intestines.

- ➢ **Exercise regularly**

    Having a good workout program prepare you on a daily basis but it still depends on what you are trying to achieve for example you are overweight and trying to lose weight then the right workout routine for you is high-intensity training, a program which is designed for losing weight.

On the other hand, if you are trying to put on some muscle mass then "bulking" workout routines is the one that you should try.

- **Motivate yourself**

    Motivation is really a great way to keep you on track and at pace. It is very crucial in your goal to have a better memory because it will give you the eagerness to continue especially when you feel that you are not having any progress at all on your goals. What I can advise you is you have to envision your goals whenever you are trying to achieve something. This is very essential when you are trying to sharpen your memory. Some of the ways for me to get some motivation is I browse motivational quotes from successful people as well as listen to motivational music and it works wonders you should try that too!

- **Do not smoke**

    The chemicals that cigarettes emit when you smoke goes inside your body which destroys the brain cells and other organs of your body particularly the lungs. Prolonged exposure to these chemicals such as nicotine that can be found in cigarettes can elevate the risk of getting Alzheimer's disease and certain types of cancers.

By following these tips and into your everyday routine I am sure that you will prevent a lot of delays in your learning process and once you successfully programmed yourself to do what is right and eventually resolved your weaknesses, I am truly sure that your memorization skills will progress.

So, you have the thought of what to do, it seems that you are now ready for the proceeding chapters of the eBook and develop your well-being with your goals of enhancing your memory. This is the main reason why you bought this eBook anyway right? That is why hold on as I unveil to you my secrets in memory enhancement!

CHAPTER 3

Do Not Believe in Lies The Mind is the Limit as Long the Mind Can Envision the Fact That You Can Do Anything Then You Can Do it

As we all know there are lots of myths that we actually believed when it comes to the functions of our brain which results in a stunt of progress when it comes to sharpening our memory.

These factors are old tales in which we believed for a long time and have passed down unto us by the previous generations. Here are some examples of these myths:

- ➢ **Games for the brain**

    This is actually a myth that most of us have believed that it completely true and because of that many of us are buying different kinds of games that are said to improve memory such as puzzles and board games.

Actually, it is not true, but what it can just do is just to train you to become more logical and it has nothing to do with your intelligence quotient. For example, if you are good at chess or solving the Rubik's cube it does not mean that you have a very high IQ. However, these types of puzzles can build up concentration and is a good mental exercise to keep you dynamic and have a recreational time that has a sense.

- **Left and Right-brained personal**

It is a long-time myth that we humans believed that there are types of ability in which we are good at rational thinking if we are "left-brained" while we are good at intuitive thinking if we are "right-brained." But the fact is there is no scientific finding to prove that claim meaning it is just hearsay and with proper training as well as experience all types of people can be good in rationalization and intuition as well.

- **Progression of our brain doesn't stop**

The truth is our brain continues to progress even if we reach adulthood and our learning is proof of that. We continue to learn new things in our everyday life here on the planet Earth which is sufficient proof already that our knowledge has a continued growth which is also part of brain development.

> **We learn because our brain cells add up.**

This is completely false! We are learning because of the knowledge that we get from our everyday experiences which makes our brain cells alive.

> **Humans only utilize the ten percent of the brain**

This is complete a hoax because a healthy person uses the whole portion of their brain.

> **Music heightens the logical ability of kids**

This belief has nothing to do with the rate of the logical thinking of children and there is no proven evidence that testifies this claim.

These are the most common myths that are taught to us by the elders since the early times. And the primary reason why this is made is for the purpose of gaining profit because of the products that are on a sale that is related to this hoax and myths. In short, these myths are just there to promote the products that are related to them.

A friendly advice

One advice that I can give you is you have to learn to choose the knowledge that is worth absorbing. You also need to have a deep foundation on how our brain is functioning this is the main intention on why I made this eBook for you to develop your memorization skills the correct and straightforward way and to keep you away from false beliefs which will just stunt your progress.

How to Unlock your Inner Potential

Here is the suggestion that I can give you if you want to notice the maximum potential of your brain which will be a huge help in obtaining spectacular memorization skills.

- ➢ **Modify your beliefs**

    Just what we have talked about a while ago which are all about myths, once you have integrated those false beliefs in your mind it will be hard for you to improve that is why one thing you can do is to remove those false beliefs and change it with the new and correct facts. By executing this you are welcoming up new opportunities for your mind especially welcome possible new learning such as what we are discussing here in this eBook which is to improve your memory.

- **Only absorb truthful knowledge**

    We are all in right age maybe except for some minors that are reading this eBook. However, the point is we can all understand what is right and what is wrong that is why you must determine what knowledge are worthy for acceptance and one example of knowledge that are worthy to be rejected our neuromyths and other old maid sayings.

- **Work hard and love what you are doing**

    When it comes to learning you will not accomplish anything if you will not keep trying. In this eBook, we are talking about the ways on how you can sharpen your memory as I am giving all the knowledge that I have which is all about the topic however if you will not put any efforts at all on improving yourself then everything that we are doing here will be useless. One thing that I can advise you is after you have obtained the knowledge does not stop from there and continue to enhance it by practicing.

➢ **Confidence**

Increasing your confidence levels is a significant way to learn everything effortlessly because a heart that is full of anxiety and low self-esteem will greatly hinder the spark of learning because you are not comfortable on your own abilities. These are the ways that you can implement in your own life to use the full capacity of your brain to perform much better and I am very sure that you can memorize things easier and your potential will have no boundaries than you can ever imagine.

CHAPTER 4

Be Here and Now

Make Things Happen Right Here Right Now

Being motivated is one of the factors on how I reached this feat in my life which is to have a "limitless memory." Because whenever I am motivated, I feel that I can do anything which I applied to my journey of having a sharp memory before.

What I do is I listen to motivational speeches and read some motivational quotes from the experts because we can get a lot of wisdom from them for the reason that they already experience a lot of hardships that is why by listening to them you will get the wisdom that they are imparting on you which you can eventually apply on your own life.

Because of that, I obtained an exceptional focus which is really great in boosting my productivity and that is a fact that is why in this chapter we will be tackling the strategies on how to make things happen.

There is this one technique that I found very effective in making things happen especially when I am demoralized this is known as the "Five More Rule". The logic in this technique is when you feel like you are restless and needs to be strong. The thing that you must do is do another five of whatever you are doing it this will give you a boost that you can do it, especially if you are losing your focus.

Five Rules

The title of the method explains the method already "Five More Rule," and it is really pretty easy to do because you will just literally implement what the name of the method states. For example, you are having a hard time on a problem particularly a physics problem because it is really difficult and you are giving up on it then implement the "Five More Rule" by grabbing another 5 physics problems and solve it all by doing this you are making your mental stability tough which will immune itself on future problems that you will be facing.

You can also implement it to other problems that you are encountering add an extra five every time you are experiencing setbacks and it will surely increase your stamina on such problems resulting to a much greater ability to solve such problems.

There is also an alternative way to achieve optimal focus which is by using your imagination, one thing that I do is to put my hands in a circle shape around my eyes and I look at the thing that I want to focus very closely, for example, I am taking an exam the next day what I look closely is the book that I suppose to read.

By doing this you are taking away all the distractions that hinder your concentration on the thing that you must accomplish.

See it is easy to concentrate on something if you have the urge to do so. Here are some of the advice that I can give you on how I maintain a deep focus on everything that I do.

- ➢ **Give yourself some type of evaluation**

    You must keep in mind the factors and things that keep your concentration away from you in this way you will be able to stay away from those distractions to bring your focus back. Some of the well-known distractions are gadgets, extracurricular activities, and etc.

- ➢ **You have to concentrate on things one point at a time**

    By doing this you will have an ample effort to be exerted on the things that you are doing and will avoid the diversion of attention from it. In this way, your performance will surely increase. It is a very important aspect to becoming good in memorization.

- ➢ **Move on from the past**

    Some of our past experiences are usually not that pleasant such broken relationships, loss of a loved one, failures, and a lot more. If you are continuously contemplating these things you will surely lose your focus every time you try to do your tasks or work.

- ➢ **It is important to have short breaks when working**

    By doing this you are giving your brain a kind of rest which will bring your focus back. For the reason that as we all know a tired and weary brain will not absorb the knowledge that you are trying to obtain.

CHAPTER 5

Create and Connect

The main reason on why we called this chapter as create and connect is because of that in order for us to memorize things we will be needing to create this memory on our mind and absorb it thoroughly so that it can eventually be stored on the memory bank.

The most crucial part is connecting this memory in the latter part whenever we want to remember them. This is where our memory will be tested especially if the memory happened a long time ago already. This will be the real challenge that accompanies the process of "remembering"

What easy to do challenges can you integrate on your daily activities to challenge your brain?

- ➢ When you are brushing your teeth, you are using a specific hand it might be the left or right. If you are used to using your left hand why not try to use, you're the other hand. In this way, your brain will work tremendously because of an unusual routine unlike if you are doing the same routine every day then everything is just passive and what only work is the muscle memory which does give any challenge to our brain at all.

- ➤ When you are having your dinner or lunch or even your breakfast you can even close your eyes while putting the food inside your mouth.
- ➤ Every morning includes a new exercise which you have not done before probably one to two minutes only.

These different activities will give a certain shock to the brain which will eventually sharpen it in the long run because these activities are also a kind of training for your brain. However, if there is no chance of doing a physical activity during that day you can go for some activities that do not require any extensive work physically such as reading a new book, play a musical instrument, or even learning a new language or dialect are really great in keeping your brain active which will give your memory the sharpness it needs.

Give a certain dare to your brain by doing these several routines that you are doing daily which are literally bad for your brain by eliminating these habits you are helping your memory to become sharper.

- ➤ Take away sugar on your diet – Sugar (especially white sugar) possess several chemicals that once you consumed a lot of sugar the glucose in your body will greatly increase which can give you a high risk of damaging your blood vessels.

- ➤ Clear away negative thoughts – This will just promote stress and eventually will become the primary reason for taking your focus away from you. As we all know to be out of focus and stress affects your brain a lot

- ➤ Never overeat – overeating can also increase the glucose levels on our body which can bring a lot of significant damage to our blood vessels and can give our gut a lot of difficulties digesting our foods.

- ➤ Meditation - This will give your brain a fresh boost from the stressful week that you have experience primarily because of school or work. It will also release stress hormones away from your body which is one of the primary causes of being out of focus which will make you more focus and alert.

- ➤ Write a diary or journal - What you can write in the journal are the positive things had happened throughout your day.

You can also include some ideas on this journal on what you will do on the next day or your goals and aspirations in life.

CHAPTER 6

Bring Information to Life

When you hear the word "bringing information to life" what comes first to your mind? Maybe a superhuman that could actually transform what he or she has in mind into a reality.

Your perception regarding that is completely false because bringing information to life is actually about your memory. This information is stored in our memory bank and we are really responsible on how we can dig it further to our own advantage

And with this technique, you can actually filter out information to avoid the brain to become "fully loaded" on a day to day basis, for example, you wake up in the morning and you will need to go to work or school. The only thing that you must concentrate on is what you will be doing on school or work by doing this all the information that you are thinking of can be successfully done by you. Especially if you are thinking of something that you must accomplish in school just like getting a perfect score on the exam thus envisioning will make it a reality eventually.

What I do to bring these pieces of information to life is by using "encoding" techniques.

Here are the following techniques

- Visual Encoding – Because we people tend to picture out what we want to remember. After we have encoded the information by visualizing it is momentarily stored on our iconic memory before being encoded into our long-term memory bank.

- Elaborative encoding – This usually happens when we are studying our lessons in our school or work as we are trying to connect certain data that we forgot on already present knowledge that we have or what we also called as "stock knowledge."

- Acoustic Encoding – This is where our sensory organs come to function such as sensory impulses, particularly with hearing. In this type of encoding, you will just associate a certain word with a word that has almost a complete resemblance particularly pronunciation when it comes to the given word and uses a short sentence to memorize the word quickly. For example the phrase "Pork on your fork" observe that we use fork (kitchen utensil) to remember the word pork (meat) and the sentence completely has sense in this way you will effectively remember a word and I have proven it because I use it before when I am still schooling and it gave great results!

- Tactile Encoding – In tactile encoding, we are using our senses such as a sense of smell and taste as well as feelings. One example that I can give you is when you are thinking of a food for you to determine the name of the food that you want to remember you have to taste it first then afterwards your neurons will send back a signal to help you in naming the food however if tasting is not possible then odor testing would be a great alternative.

- Semantic Encoding – This is a very basic type of memory encoding as it classifies the term for you to remember it. One example of it is knowing that a basketball is a kind of sport.

The Process of Memory Encoding

We all know that this encoding technique is a complex process as what we have discussed earlier that is why we will try our best to discuss it in an easy to understand manner.

- The process begins with perception. It is where the systematized, recognition, and understanding of the sensory details for you to comprehend the given details.

- The perception contains hints that go all the way through the nervous system which triggers the activation of the sensory system. However, perception can be classified into two processes:

- It is the where sensory input which converts low-level details to higher-level details which results to the absorption of the details into your memory bank.

- This is related to human's impressions and probabilities that persuade perception.

- After this, the perceived information is decrypted into the different portions of the cortex and will be merged in the hippocampus into a sole experience. Then the hippocampus will decide whether where it will be placed either on short or long-term memory.

For you to understand more there are different levels on where memory encoding can happen such as:

- Short-term memory – This is where momentary information is placed inside our brain. The common things that are stored as a short-term memory are quick tasks such as carrying this bag or writing certain sentences on a paper. These types of incidence will typically last for several minutes only.

- Long-term memory – This is where infinite storage of information is placed and most of the time it is the incidents in our lives that leave a significant mark on our personalities such as our name, the place we live, our family, and many events such as marriage and etc.

Transferring information from Short-Term Memory to Long-term Memory

If given a chance to transfer bits of information from our short-term memory to our long-term memory? Then it would be amazing as we can remember things for a much extended period of time.

Is it possible and if yes how can we do it?

Yes, it is fully possible with the help of a certain part of our brain it is achievable. So, this is so-called "amygdala" must be engaged in order for the short-term memory to be transferred to the long-term memory bank.

So, what are the ways that you can do in order for it to happen?

- ➤ **Repetition – This is a very important technique that must be done if you want to transfer the information from your short-term memory bank to your long-term memory bank. Also, the inclusion of your emotions while repeating the terms that you want to transfer to your long-term memory will be a huge help for the quick transfer this is the only way that you can use in order for you to transfer the information as you cannot negate the natural physiological process of our brain.**

After all that now you have the insight of what encoding looks like because I made it before simple to understand without putting scientific terms which will just delay your learning because you did not buy this eBook just to become an anatomist or a doctor but you bought this eBook to help you in your memory enhancement journey.

CHAPTER 7

Use Your Body to Remember

What I will teach you in this chapter is how to memorize different kinds of things using your body parts.

We will be using our ten body parts and we will start from our:

- head
- ears
- eyes
- nose
- mouth
- chin
- armpit
- belly
- knees
- feet

The Process:

- The first thing that I would like you to envision chopsticks on your mind. There is a chopstick on top of my head and ready to pick up some sushi any time.
- Next, we are down in the ears then imagine an Indian curry dish and the sauce is overflowing and coming out of your ears.
- Then a burger that is coming out of your eyes.
- Then on the nose visualize that someone is pressing dough in front of your nose and I want you to remember the word "in the dough."
- Next is visualize a bra that is coming out of your mouth than in the chin, there are playing cards coming out of it and the card dealer is just getting an infinite number of cards on your chin.
- Then raise your armpit and imagine that your armpit is giving out some kind of cereal called "cheerios".
- Next is the belly button, imagine that a gun is there and just firing random shots of belly buttons everywhere and the sound that it makes is "bang."
- Then on your knees imagine that there is a glass of vodka.

- ➢ And on the floor imagine that there is a cooking pan.
- ➢ Now try to remember everything from the top and see how it goes.

What did We just Did?

Maybe you are not aware that you have just memorized the top ten most populated countries in the world.

Here is the proof:

- ➢ Chopsticks = China
- ➢ Indian curry = India
- ➢ Hamburger = USA
- ➢ In dough = Indonesia
- ➢ Bra = Brazil
- ➢ Pack of cards = Pakistan
- ➢ Cheerios = Nigeria
- ➢ Bang = Bangladesh
- ➢ Vodka = Russia
- ➢ Pan = Japan

CHAPTER 8

Pegging Information Down

After the data is processed by our senses and eventually sent to our brain as we have said in the previous chapter it will choose to go either on the short-term or long-term memory. Once it was stored there the next problem is how can you retrieve that information accurately?

This is where consolidation will take place because it engraves a certain footprint on our brain whenever we are receiving information. Every information passes through this consolidation stage, this is very crucial whenever we are thinking of something that we want to reminisce.

For example, it is dinner time and we want to remember what you have eaten on your lunchtime this is where our brain consolidates all the information that is inside our "memory bank." It will recollect all the information and will come up on the most possible answer to your inquiry.

In consolidation, complete hours of sleep are very important as it promotes the good development of consolidation in our memory it also rejuvenates the activation patterns on our brain for a much better consolidation it is also said that in the first few hours of sleep the latest memories that are stored in our brain are solidified.

But there are people who claim that they are having a hard time memorizing stuff. Yes, there are people with such claims but it is probably true for some people who have medical conditions such as dementia and Alzheimer's disease. However, for people who are completely healthy it is probably because of personal reasons such examples are written below:

- **The person may not have absorbed the information clearly.**
- **The person might not put any emphasis on the information because of that it is not truly stored in the "memory bank."**
- **The person has a hard time retrieving the information accurately because of the lack of information regarding the subject.**

So, let's get down deep on memory consolidation for you to deeply understand the subject.

Process of Memory Consolidation

Because in the process of memory consolidation the neurons in our brain use the event of long-term potentiating which permits a synapse to have an elevated strength as the heightened numbers of the signal are sent among the 2 neurons.

Neurons and their Importance

Also called as brain cells it is a cell that somehow "electrical" in a way that it uses an electronic-like process in our brain to process and send out information. It is said that the average human possesses 100 billion neurons. Another fact about neuron is that it never divides or diminishes, unlike other cells.

These neurons are irreplaceable meaning once they are lost it will be already gone for good. Neurons are also interconnected with other neurons in our brain that is why it is very crucial for each one of them to work properly because if one of those neurons fails the process in our brain will be affected as well and plays a huge role in our memory retrieval.

Memory Retrieval

It is the action in which we try to access what happened in the PAST and those memories are located in our memory bank. These memories are previously encoded on our memory bank and the only thing that we humans can reminisce those details is by having healthy neurons.

When we want to reminisce something, we are thinking of it so deeply that is why there is no significant difference between remembering and thinking. And once we successfully reminisced of something that we want to remember it is always persistent that it is always not completely the same with original have you observed that?

Simply because there are also other items that your neurons are also processing such as the mere fact that you are thinking while you are remembering something is also a process.

CHAPTER 9

Linking Thoughts

Our human brain is one spectacular part of our body. But how do we link the thoughts that are coming inside our minds? Are you aware that most of the memory that we remember is by a process which is called "direct retrieval"?

Direct Retrieval

This is where parts of our memory are interconnected through an inquiry and not by scanning a series of events that had happened in the past just like what computers execute when they want to retrieve information they would scan the files deeply unlike indirect retrieval in which we are basing on inquiries.

To conclude, the most effective way to consolidate the information accurately on your brain is by avoiding any distractions so that your brain will not have a hard time processing the information.

Process of Memory Retrieval

For you to have a background of the process of memory retrieval I will break it down to you in simpler terms. Because I believe that in order for you to have a sharp memory you have to fully understand first how the process goes.

First step: It starts when a person wants to remember a certain event, person, or an object.

Second Step: The person will start to make inquiries on their mind such as "When and where did it happen?" and "What happened?".

Third Step: The person will start to visualize what he recollects on his or her mind.

This is where our mind will decide what method it will use in order to access the memory bank. There are two methods that it can consider namely "recognition" and "recall".

Difference between Recognition and Recall

When it comes to recognizing a person tends to link an incident or a physical entity that a person has experienced this will be the basis of the mind to recollect each and every detail of the memory that a person is trying to remember.

On the other hand, recall is actually a little bit different because when a person chooses to retrieve memory in this method, he or she will be reminiscing the memory by using an occurrence or a thing that is not handy right now.

So, which is better between the two?

When it comes to accuracy recognition works best for most of us in memory retrieval simply because it only needs a basic "familiarity decision"."

The memory will undergo again a two-step process in which weighing in the choices is required to come up with a decision of "what is it?" or "what happened?"

In this step, the neurons are also reconstructing the details of the memory and in need for an "activation" of the neurons that have the responsibility on that specific memory.

See that's how amazing our brain works!

This is where the consolidated information will come together to form one concrete copy of the real thing. For example, a while ago you are trying to remember the face of a beautiful woman that you met a while ago and with the previous process, your mind has recollected the place you met the woman, her clothes, and lastly her facial features.

Process of Recall

Now you know that recognition is one powerful process, it is also crucial to know the other one which is a recall. There are three types of recall:

- Free recall – this is where a person has been handed out an outline of items to remember and requested to recall them in any order. This is actually common in schools as we all know our teachers before are always giving us terms to memorize and we tend to contemplate on them for several minutes especially on graded recitations or even days (depends on the length) then recite it in front of the class. I know we are all frightened by that situation right?
- Cued recall – this type is almost the same with free recall however the only difference is instead of recalling the items in any order, the person will be tried with the utilization of

guides. Because of this, it guides the person to successfully remember the items that are in the outline that is given to him. Most of the items in the outline are totally diminish because they are forgotten or not completely absorb by the brain and the guide acts as a hint for the person to recall the specific object. One example that I can give you is we are trying to recall an object and we forgot it completely we can think of something that resembles it or ask someone to give us a clue such as the first letter of the word of the object is truly beneficial in remembering it.

- Serial recall – this would be the most complex type of recall this is where we must recognize and remember the objects in an outline in their corresponding chronological order. But do not worry because I will help you throughout your way to achieving such feat.

Here are the tips for you to achieve a successful serial recall:

- If possible, concentrate on the latest events in this way you can shrink the number of objects/events to be remembered.
- You can also recall the objects in a different order first and just arrange them chronologically afterward.
- There will times when a recurrence error would occur but do not mind it because it happens from time to time.

Life Example

Actually, making those memories to be stored long-term what you need to do is you need to rehearse the act more for example below is a given number random telephone number:

800708204

What can you observe on that number aside from it is composed of nine digits? It is more difficult to memorize right? Because the numbers are condensed and the tendency is you will read it as a whole which will compromise the ability to easily absorb the digits to your mind.

How about if we put the writing of this digit this way?

800-708-204

What can you notice? I divided the 9-digit telephone number into three parts, this way when I am going to memorize it what I will do is I will memorize it by parts in this way I the brain will not have a hard time absorbing the digits which will be eventually absorbed on my long-term memory storage.

See? Memory encoding is just easy with the proper knowledge and techniques that you will further learn in this eBook you can easily memorize anything under the sun. That technique is just a glimpse of the techniques that you will learn here and in the following chapter, I will elaborate more about memory storage and how we can retrieve the memories that are currently stored in our memory bank.

Secrets to Memorize Faster than Anyone

Have you watched the movie Limitless? If you have you probably remember the protagonist who found a special pill that allowed him to remember almost everything such as experience and knowledge when he needed to if this were applicable to real life it would be a very weird thing right?

We, humans, tend to forget a lot of data and do you have an idea why does it occur and how we can manage to make our memory sharper. Because our brain is like a hard drive of a computer, it has limited storage space and our brain is a very excellent sorting machine that filters out irrelevant information by storing it on our short-term memory that is why if you do not repeat it you will forget it very quickly. Here are some of the tips that you can use.

- Learn the most necessary information only

- Switch your attention from one topic to another and not to that sole topic for a long period of time because your brain gets used to the information that you are putting inside that is why you must always give the brain a kind of a "shock" by placing new information from different topics if this is not possible a quick rest or play musical instruments are great alternative.

- If possible, avoid similar information because it can get mixed and cause confusion.

- Use "Nail words" for example you are trying to memorize the word nail you have to connect it using your fingers by thinking of other words that are related to it such as wall, hammer, and door.

CHAPTER 10

Remembering Names

We all know that remembering names can be tough especially if you do not know the person personally but there are a lot of ways that I can teach you how to remember them the easy way.

Only relying on one part of your brain will just give you limited powers. Just like the superheroes that we are reading in comic books they push themselves to the limits to ensure that everything is under their control. It is like our brains if only one part of it is working then our progress and capacity are limited only and one thing that I have observed is that activating the two parts of our brain namely the left and the right hemispheres gives us the power that we need in memorizing effectively. This is what I use in my 15-minute training routines every day and I really benefited from it because I can now easily remember any names and terms in just a short period of time. So, in this chapter, you will know how to remember names effectively and at the same time how to activate the two parts of your brain.

Effectively use of Left and Right Brain for Memorization

There are lots of benefits of using the left and right brain to become effective in memorization. I actually recommend it because of it I can memorize everything in just 15 minutes (depends on the volume). So here are the techniques that I am using in using my both sides of my brain:

- ➢ Do not rely on logic only –simply because if you are going to use only your logic in making decisions you will just only use a part of your thinking capacity because of that only one side of your brain is functioning. Instead, try to gather more facts before making a decision in this way your brain will be using its maximum capacity and will supply any missing information that is needed which will benefit you in the long run.

- ➢ Use visualizations – while memorizing draw images in your mind that are related to what you are thinking because of this you are practicing both sides of your brain to cooperate with each other.

- ➢ Get yourself involve with numbers – this is a great way to train your left brain if you are not fond of interacting with numbers. By training your left brain you are also giving your brain a chance to have an active two hemispheres thus resulting in good working relationship of the two hemispheres of your brain.

- Find a hobby – if you are left-brained this is very crucial because this will enhance your right brain because you are using your creativity here which makes both parts of your brain to work in the long run.

See you will not have to pay anything to achieve good memorization skills you just have to use the resources that are already given to you and apply these techniques that I have taught you.

Quick Methods

Choose one of the methods and do it for a minimum of 15 minutes every day (you can use a different method every day) because our goal here is to train your memorization skills.

- 1st Method: Say again the name of a person a little bit loud after they introduced their name to you by doing this you are putting a strong imprint on your memory bank to retain that information for a much longer period of time.

- 2nd Method: Request the person who newly introduced themselves to you to spell out their name. By doing this you are having a good visualization of their name. Also, by spelling out the name of the person to you, you will have ample time to absorb their name which will bring in a big chance for that memory to be stored long term. One trick for you to successfully get their permission to repeat their name is by telling them "I did not hear it clearly; can you spell it out for me?" Trust me it works every time.

- 3rd Method: Link the name of the person base on a fact about him. This is a pretty good method especially if you know a lot about the person. However, this is not advisable for people that you have just met once except that if they have a very distinct feature, for example, a weird facial feature or disability.

- 4th Method: Reiterate the name of the person in your head. This is a great way to establish the name on your memory bank. One trick that you can add up to make it extra effective is by over overstress the syllables, segregate it into smaller portions, or you can also apply the previous methods such as link it to other words.

- 5th Method: Link the name of the person to a person that is related to your life. For example, if the name of the person that you want to remember the name is the same with the name of your brother or sister even if the name is not exactly the same word for word but the actual resemblance of the name to each other is a big plus already.

- For example : The name of the person that you want to remember is Darla and you have a sister named Carla then you can link Darla to Carla if you want to remember Darla the person that you newly met.

- 6th Method: Find a common ground on the person that you newly met. I really found this very effective because whenever you have a common interest with a person you will not have a hard time remembering that person's name.

- 7th Method: Make an acronym of the person's name. For example, you have a newly met classmate named Derek you can give that guy an acronym for his name for you to easily remember it the acronym that you can give is "Dude Enjoys Extensive Kickboxing."

- 8th Method: Produce a picture of the person in your mind by linking it with other things. For example, you have met a girl named Crystal the next thing you should do is to imagine a beautiful crystal ring to remember her name easily.

- 9th Method: Find a unique feature of the person. This will allow your mind to easily grasp the information on your memory bank whenever you need them.

- 10th Method: Picture out a weird scene. For example, you have a met a guy who works at a doll store imagine him that he is in a place that is full of dolls in which the dolls are as big as him, alive and talking to him.

Ron White's Method

In this method, Ron White reiterated that it will be a huge help in memorizing names if you link the name of a person to an object that has a similar sound with their name and pictures out the object on your mind as well for an optimal effect.

For example:

You met a girl named Abby you can link it with the words "A bee" and by visualizing a picture of a bee on your mind you will establish a strong imprint on your memory bank for easy remembrance of the name.

Harry Lorayne's Method

With these rules, you can make it sure that you are having a consistent guideline in remembering names. Here are the following rules:

➤ Hear the name very carefully.
➤ Spell out the name.
➤ Create a unique remark about the name.
➤ Utilize the name on your first conversation with the person.
➤ Utter the name of the person before you part ways with each other.

Right now, you know that there are a lot of methods that you can choose from if you want to memorize the name of a person effectively. Just learn to find what method best fits you.

*NOTE: Mix these rules with the exercises for combining the left and right brain hemispheres for more optimal results.

For you to remember names of people easily for the long-term you have to do the techniques for at least 15 minutes a day to keep your mind guessing and for you to have the mastery of the techniques that will enhance your memorization skills you can only use 1 to 2 techniques per day. Also, you can choose what works best for you and you can alternate the techniques for you to have a variation

CHAPTER 11

Remember the Number

Usually, people are having difficulties memorizing numbers for the reason that they are simply allergic to numbers or literally just do not want to deal with them. Since I was a kid, I was not a fan of math subjects that is why I really did not want to deal on them too. I just gained interest with them when I started to have the urge in enhancing my memorizing skills. So here are the techniques that I use when I want to remember a certain number.

➢ **Use shapes as a symbol for you to remember a number**

2	Duck
10	Plate and bread knife

➢ **The phonetic system**

1	t d
2	n
3	m
4	R
5	L

6	j, sh, ch
7	k g
8	f v
9	p b
0	z s

- **Link sounds to digits** – this usually efficient with shorter numbers.

    I. First, you must allocate a consonant sound or sound for

    II. Every number, as long as you utilize the identical sounds for the identical number every time.

    III. If you do not feel like taking time to produce your own scheme, you also use an existing one that you have created before.

    IV. But vowel sounds do not have a place on this method because it is difficult to associate digits to their sounds.

- **Produce words using the sounds** – produce words using the sounds allocated to each digit. The examples are on the table below:

4918217	r-b-d/t/th-v/f-n-d/t/th-k/c/g to 491 – robot 82 – fan 17 - dog

Afterward, you can visualize the words that you have created into real-life images for you to get the most out of this method.

Memorizing the Pi

A person who has memorized the pi is really remarkable and your friends will surely be amazed after they saw your skill in memorization. I also memorized the pi easily with the technique that I will be teaching you here.

Method 1 – Grouping

- Generate a chart
- 3.141 5926 5358 9793 2384 6264 3383
- Memorize the groups one step at a time – by doing this you are preventing "information overload" and confusion. This will also guarantee a more effective memorization result.

➤ Scale it up afterward, once you already memorized the 3 to 4 groups target 5 to 6 groups and so on.

➤ If you have a friend or family that has the same number with one of the groups that you created for pi then list it down on a piece of paper to give you an added guide or if none get 3 groups of number from pi for example 314 159 26543 and try to create a telephone number-like order like (314)159-2653 then start to memorize it and to make the memorization process faster name those telephone number-like groups with a name from a real person.

Method 2 – Word & Sound Swap

Write a sentence that corresponds to the number of letters that a digit in pi represents for example:

➤ 3 = Now

➤ 1 = I

➤ 4 = will

➤ 1 = a

➤ 5 = rhyme

➤ 9 = construct

- ➢ 2 = by
- ➢ 5 = letter

Note: Grammar structure is not a factor here as long as the sentence's thought is clear you are all set. You can also construct a poem out of it whatever makes you comfortable is great and a lot of people are having a lot of success in rhyming too by producing a song out of it for easier memorization of twinkle twinkle little star is a popular song that most people use to rhyme in number-sound swapping to memorize pi.

Combination of Left & Right Brain for Better Memorization

Our brain is separated into two different major parts which are left and right hemispheres and different chunks of information go inside them. However, they are always in contrast with each other and work differently and by combining them it rests assured that your memory skills will become sharper as well.

Here are some ways that you can do to activate both sides of your brain immediately:

- Do juggling – even though you are not good at juggling balls it only takes practice to learn it. And why should you learn it? Simply because juggling requires eye and brain coordination and the more balls that you jug our brain will be required to use its two hemispheres to react quickly to what is happening as you juggle.

- Use different colored pens – this is pretty simple and will not require any training at all. All you have to do is write down the word of a color using a different color of a pen. In this way, the two parts of your brain will be activated.

- Example - Write the word yellow on a piece of paper with a blue pen and do this also for other colors as well such as write the word green with the use of a red pen and so on.

Devout a few minutes for these exercises every day and you will see a lot of difference in your improvement. I have been using these for several years now and it works wonders for my brain. I suggest you add these methods to your daily routine and practice it for at least 15 minutes a day and I tell you that you will greatly improve in terms of memorization.

CHAPTER 12

Art of Memory

When it comes to sharpening your memorization skills you can use these techniques that also involves your spirituality as well because it teaches you to persevere and to use your mind to cooperate with your overall being and the most amazing thing here is you do not have to spend any money in order for you to master memorization. Everything is provided and you can do it yourself that is why this eBook is called as "Limitless Memory." Because I believe that you do not have to spend a lot of money in drinking different supplements and hire an instructor to enhance your memory throughout the way for the reason that everything can be done by yourself and by following the techniques that I am and I will be teaching here in this eBook.

Memory Palace Technique

One of the most sought techniques is known as the "Memory Palace" it is a great technique that really helped me developed my memorization skills it is originated on the mindset of "you are exceptionally good in reminiscing the places that you know." It is a representation of a place you know it could be your home or your office on where you are working this will be your guide throughout the process of "Memory Palace Technique"

This is how it is done:

> **Choose your Palace**

    The first thing that you will do is to select a place that you are really familiar with. The precision of this technique will be based on your capacity to visualize and stroll in that place comfortably. You would be in that place using your mind only.

    One concrete example is your home because you are residing there for an extended period of time that is why you are really familiar with the place. Next thing that you will do is to recall each item according to their order in your house.

> **Take note of the unique features**

    In this step, you will need to become aware of the unique features of your house, for example, an elegant chandelier. After that continue strolling on the memory palace.

Check the different rooms that are inside the memory palace and take note of the striking features of that room on your mind. Each of those will become slots in your memory which you will use to place every piece of data you accumulated.

➢ **Memory Palace Imprint**

Visual-oriented people have a lot of advantage when it comes to this step because you will imprint what you have seen in your mind inside your memory bank. Here are some tips that I can give you when it comes to this step:

- ✓ Stroll on the route physically by doing it you are making your memorization easier also say again the unique features as you are viewing them.

- ✓ Get a piece of paper and jot down the features and visualize them again on your mind and at the same time repeating those features with the use of your mouth.

- ✓ You can repeat these steps until you master the step.

- **Application**

  - ✓ After you have mastered the previous steps it is now ready to be applied on the real life. For example, you need to do the grocery this time and wanted to do it without using a list then you can use my previous example when we use our house as a memory palace, we can associate each of the items that we will buy on the grocery on any object for us to memorize it easily.

  - ✓ One example is when you want to buy an egg you can associate it with a picture of your mother. So that is the idea you have to learn how to associate each item for another object for you to easily understand it.

Acronyms

This is one of the easiest methods in enhancing your memory and most of all it is the most commonly used especially by beginners. So how does this method go? It is just easy, here it goes for every word that you want to memorize you just have to take the first letter up to the last letter of that word and think of a catchy phrase or word for you to remember that word easily, for example, the word smile you can give it some color by putting up some acronym on it:

S pecial

M agic

I n

L iving

E veryday

Now you know what I am talking about you now saw that it is much easier to memorize because of the catchy phrase that you associated with it!

The Method of Loci

This is one of my most favorite techniques in memorization. This method is already present even on the ancient ages, particularly in Rome. It is first heard on one of the works of Cicero which are called as the "De Oratore".

This method uses picturing out information with the use of recognizable information about a specific environment to speed up the process of remembering.

There are a lot of memorization competitions back in the day that uses different objects to remember information. The objects that they used are but not limited to parts of their body, numbers, and outline of words.

This method will be a complete advantage if you are exceptional in visualization. Here is one concrete example the method for you to deeply absorb the knowledge that I am talking about here.

- ➢ Think of a place that you are very familiar with, such as your own dwelling place.
- ➢ Imagine a number of areas in the place in a rational order. For an instance imagine the way you usually go into your house to reach the back door from the front door.
- ➢ Start at the front door and proceed through the hallway, go into the living, dining room, and the bedroom you can add up more different areas in your house if you want as well as functional room, kitchen or even the dirty kitchen if you want.

➢ Because when you wish to reminisce objects, just imagine your house and go through the different specific places inside your home all by visualization.

➢ If you are going to the grocery and would want to remember the things that you will be buying without the help of a list this would be very beneficial.

➢ For example, you would want to buy an insect spray, corned beef, and a sausage. Visualize it as you push the button of the spray on your front door the smell of it will be all over the front door this smell will be imprinted on your mind which will result to a much effective remembering,

➢ Now continue your way inside the house and visualize seven-foot-tall sausage in a bun that wears a headdress such as a hat in the living room. As you go further the house, you saw a fat corned beef that wears a sunglass in the dining room.

Now it is time for you to try it out. I am always implementing this when I have to buy something, the more unique and unusual you associate the item the better results to you can get.

Other Useful Techniques

I know you got a piece of the awesome techniques that I know and I would share more of the memorization techniques because I really want you to enhance your memorization skills because I know that you can use it for your own good. Here are more techniques that I use in improving my memorization skills.

Mnemonic – in this technique a short poem or a unique word is utilized to aid a person to reminisce a thing. Below is a complete example of mnemonic:

Please	P	Parenthesis
Excuse	E	Exponent
My	M	Multiplication
Dear	D	Division
Aunt	A	Addition
Suzy	S	Subtraction

That is just one example of a simple word mnemonic technique. However, mnemonic technique actually has eight more types meaning you have a lot more choices depends on your preference and what works best for you.

- **Music mnemonics** – Have you observed that when people are repeating songs over and over again, they could actually memorize it easier? Simply because our minds much prefer to tackle sentences that are pleasant to the ears because of this we tend to repeat them again and again which makes us memorize the sentences easier.

Example:

When children sing the alphabet (A, B,C) they memorized it easier because of the song.

- **Name mnemonics** – this is where the first letter of the word of the items are used to form a name acronym that has an equivalent catchy phrase to remember the list easily.

Example: ROY G. BIV – Red, Orange, Yellow, Green, Blue, Indigo, Violet

- **Model mnemonics** – this is where an existing chart is replaced with words that are needed to be memorized.

Example:

If you are memorizing the chemical table of elements you can use an existing science chart such as photosynthesis in helping you to memorize some of the table elements.

- **Ode mnemonics – in this type of mnemonics the terms that a person wants to memorize are put into a form of a poem.**

For example, you want to memorize the number of days of months you can say it this way.

30 days of September April, June, and November

All the others have 31

Except for February my beautiful daughter

Oh only 28 but it is alright except leap year it has 29

- **Note organization mnemonics – in this type of mnemonics the use of notes is greatly encouraged which promotes better memorization.**
- **Outline mnemonics – by separating the different terms that a person wants to memorize into categories for much easier and less complex absorbing of the words. In this way, the brain is**

giving an ample amount of time to familiarize the words for much easier memorization.

- Image mnemonics – this is a mnemonic technique that uses weird images to help remember a certain word.
- Connection mnemonics – this is almost the same with word linking as we have discussed in the previous chapters it is where we look for an object that we already knew and connect it to the word that we are going to memorize.

For example, we are going to memorize the direction of longitude and latitude we can remember it by thinking that there is a letter N in the word longitude and it is in the North and in contrast there is no letter N in the word latitude that is why it is not from the north,

- Spelling mnemonics – this mnemonic technique plays around with the spelling of the word that you want to memorize for easier grasping of the term.

Example:

You want to memorize the word principal and your principal before in your school was your pal.

Peg system – this technique is often used in memorizing the list. The process involves an outline of words that are very simple to link with the numbers that they rhyme with.

Some examples are written below

One	Bun
Two	Coupe
Three	Free
Four	Door
Five	Live
Six	Bricks
Seven	Heaven
Eight	Weight
Nine	Dine
Ten	Pen

Major system – in this technique the numbers are changed initially into the sounds of consonants and eventually adding vowels into it to easily memorize the words.

0	s z
1	t
2	n
3	m
4	r
5	l
6	d
7	k c g q
8	f v

CHAPTER 13

The Methods I Personally Used & Recommend

The methods below are the personal methods that I use in achieving a limitless memory.

Please refer to the methods below:

- Connect Method – this is likely similar to the methods that we discuss previously because in this method we are linking a certain item or term to images.

- Story Method – this is quite similar to the connect method however in this method you produce various images among the two items and you will mix everything into one big picture.

- Repeated Recitation – reading is a good way to master the lesson and memorize the terms but the most effective way of doing it is by reciting it loud. Have you observed that if you are reciting out the terms it is much easier for you to memorize than reading? Simply because terms are imprinted much deeper in your memory bank if you are talking to yourself.

- Learn the lesson per parts – in this way you will brain will not have a hard time absorbing the lessons.

- Learning by spaced and un-spaced – putting intervals while studying the lessons to give time to your brain to rest and become more efficient as well as this kind of strategy gives the information that you have accumulated a chance to be imprinted to the long-term memory bank.

- Intention to remember - first if you plan to memorize something you must dedicate yourself to it and do not just do it for the sake of obligation but always put it into your heart.

I am truly sure that if you implement these methods/techniques to your memorization routine I am truly sure that you will have a better progression when it comes to memorizing. I have proven these techniques to be really effective while I am still studying.

CHAPTER 14

Self-Discipline

I trace my success in achieving a limitless memory by practicing tremendous self-discipline. Because of this, I managed to learn all the knowledge that I need to possess a limitless memory. Below is my everyday morning routine that I do in my free time. In this routine, you can see how to determine I am to achieve success.

The process is called as the space repetition in this technique we repeat the words that we want to remember with the use of the pattern below.

TO MEMORIZE QUICKLY	
1st repetition 2nd repetition 3rd repetition 4th repetition	Immediately after learning After 15 to 20 minutes After 6 to 8 hours After 1 day
TO MEMORIZE FOR THE LONG TERM	

1st repetition	Immediately after learning
2nd repetition	After 20 to 30 minutes
3rd repetition	After 1 day
4th repetition	After 2 to 3 weeks
5th repetition	After 2 to 3 months

Recommendation & Tips for Memorizing

➤ Set priorities. - If you are learning a new language try to study it day and night.

➤ Recording works like magic - you can listen to it if you want to master the one that you are studying to refresh your mind.

➤ High-quality materials - to ensure that knowledge that you are getting is correct and legit.

➤ Be brave – if your mindset is like this, I am sure that you will be successful in enhancing your memorization skills as long as you will not give up and continue practicing with the help of the guides and tips that are inside this eBook you are on the right track.

➤ <u>Confidence</u> and love for what you are doing – because most of the time your first choice is the right choice that is why in

deciding what to answer on your quizzes, interviews, and etc. learn to follow what your heart says and never hesitate.

That's it! I know that you learned a lot of things in this eBook that will help you in your journey in enhancing your memorization skills and it is now time to implement these techniques in your life.

Conclusion

To conclude, achieving a limitless memory requires hard work and perseverance. Along with the methods it is very important also to change your attitude towards improving yourself because it is a very crucial factor for you to endure that challenges that these techniques might give you.

All the methods that I knew are listed, what you have to do now is to choose a method that works best for you because we are two different people that is why a method might work for me and not for you that is why you must learn to test each method and in the end decide on what method will you be using for the long run. The good with this is there are lots of methods that are listed in this eBook that is why you will not get stuck on one method alone which will make your learning experience more satisfying and enjoyable.

www.ingramcontent.com/pod-product-compliance
Lightning Source LLC
Chambersburg PA
CBHW030951240526
45463CB00016B/2449